YOUR OCEANOGRAPHY ADVENTURE

With this oceanography-themed activity book from Pangea Institute for grade four and above, you'll learn about the oceans and seas with interactive adventures and brain teasers that sharpen your skills in a fun and engaging way.

We'll travel around the world learning about bodies of salt water, how they move and the ways that they relate to the continents.

WHAT IS A OCEANOGRAPHER?

Oceanography is the branch of Earth science that studies the oceans and seas.

Many people use the terms "ocean" and "sea" as if they mean the same thing. Namely, a large body of salt water. But, there is a difference between the two terms when talking about oceanography. Seas are smaller than oceans and are located where the land and ocean meet most of the time. But, this is not always the case. Some seas are surrounded by land or "land-locked" -- just like a very big fresh water lake. However, this too is not always the case. For example, The large Great Salt Lake in North America and Lake Van in Turkey are salty, but are not called "Seas."

The oceans are very large, much larger than a sea, and the environment they represent is also very large. Thus, the science of oceanography must be just as large.

An oceanographer is a special kind of scientist that studies a variety of subject areas. He or she might focus on the ocean's biology, its chemistry, physics, geology, engineering, mathematics, computer science, or meteorology.

Oceanography scientists work together around the world to increase our knowledge of the global oceans and educate people about the ocean's processes.

So, we will look into a wide range of topics, including marine life and ecosystems, ocean circulation, plate tectonics and the geology of the sea floor, and the chemical and physical properties of the ocean in this workbook.

FUN WITH GEOGRAPHY

THE OCEANS

BY SCOTT C. MARLOWE

Cover by Scott Marlowe

First published in the United States by Pangea Press

Pangea Press
514 Winter Terrace
Winter Haven, FL
33881

ISBN: 978-1536814378

COLOR THE OCEANOGRAPHER!

OCEANS OF THE WORLD

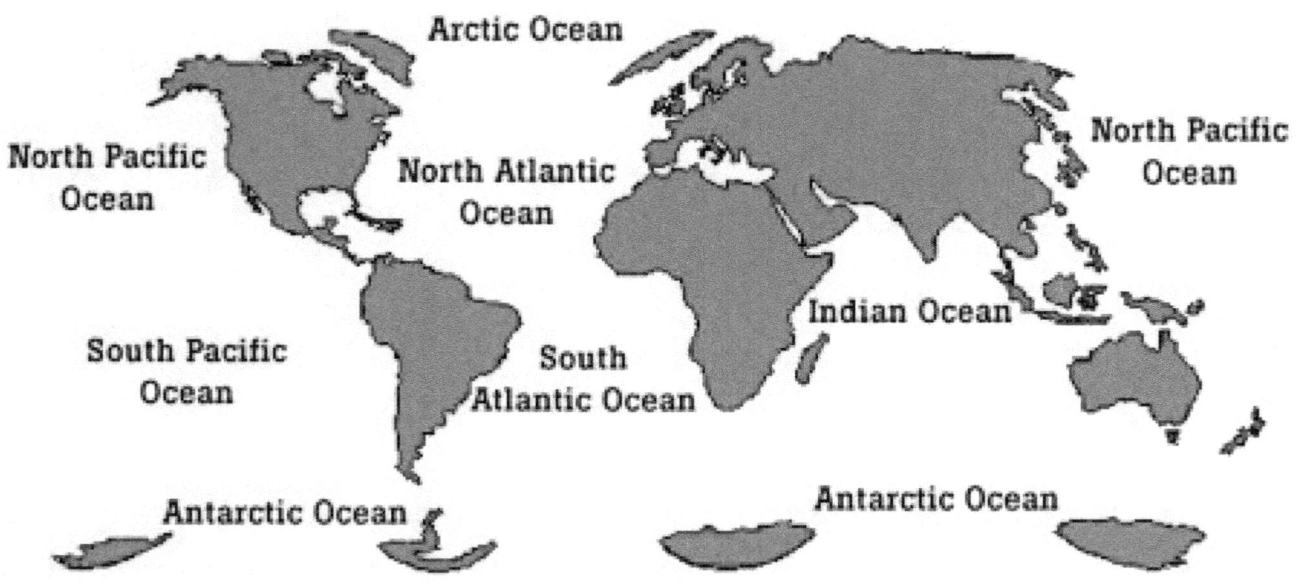

The surface of the Earth is covered with about 71% water. The water is divided by land masses called "continents" (see my other workbook on continents for more information on those).

There are five (5) oceans:

The Pacific Ocean is the largest of the Earths's oceans. It is so large that we divide it into two parts. The dividing line is the Equator which separates the Pacific into the North Pacific and South Pacific.

The next largest is the Atlantic Ocean which separates the continents of North America and South America from Europe and Africa. Like the Pacific Ocean, the Atlantic is also divided into two parts: The North Atlantic and the South Atlantic.

Then there is the Indian Ocean which is south of the continent of Asia, North of Antarctica, east of Africa, and West of Australia.

The Antarctic Ocean surrounds Antarctica and is south of the Atlantic and Pacific Oceans. And finally the Arctic Ocean which is north of Asia, Europe, and North America.

COLOR THE SAILING SHIP

WHERE DID THE OCEANS COME FROM?

Scientists have determined that Earth's oceans have existed for almost as long as the planet itself. At this time, Scientists think that there are two possible answers (called "Theories:) to explain where the oceans came from:

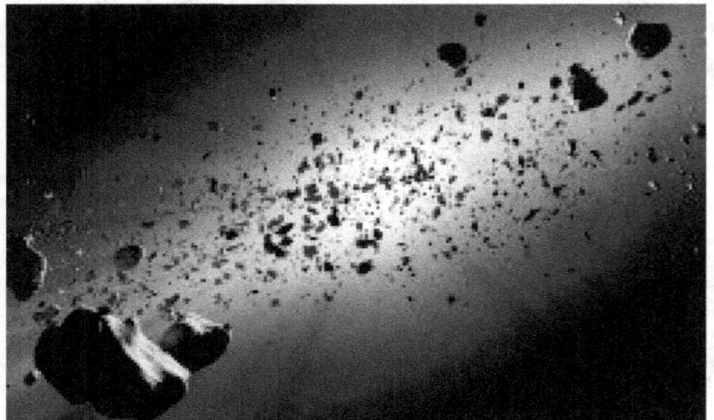

One idea says that oceans came to Earth when it was hit by many comets.

A comet is a space body made up of rock and frozen water. Many, many of them orbit the Sun and there were lots more of them when the Earth was very young.

Sometimes they ran into the earth. When this happened, the water in them was released. Over time, all the millions of collisions filled up the Oceans with their water.

Another thought is that the water came from deep inside the earth.

It was released to the surface of the planet when volcanoes erupted and spewed out hot steam along with lava and other gases.

This means that the water on the Earth was in the rocky meteorites that collided and formed the Earth right from its beginnings.

But, because of the great heat caused by the collisions, the water remained largely trapped in the rock until the planet began to cool so it could condense into the liquid state it is in today.

Either way, it seems that scientist's agree tha the Earth's water came from outer space.

WHAT'S LIES UNDER ALL THAT WATER?

The area under the Oceans is a lot like the surface of the Continents. The sea floor has open plains, valleys between mountains, canyons, deep gorges, and even volcanoes -- just like on the land.

Near the coast of each continent is the shallow continental shelf. This shelf slopes down to a plain, that is often 4,000 metres below sea level.

On the plain are deep cracks called ocean canyons or "trenches," and raised areas called ridges where the magma from the center of the Earth oozes up and pushes the tetonic plates on which the continents lay apart.

This is where you will find most, but not all, of the volcanoes in the oceans. Not all seas contain these same features.

The Ocean or Sea floor are a valuable resource because it has deposits of sediments that often have economic importance. In some places companies mine for lime, sand, phosphates, nitrates, and gravel that are used in the construction and fertilizer industries as well as other useful minerals. In other areas oil companies drill into the Earth below the water to get at oil reserves.

Yet another geological feature under the Oceans and Seas are gas hydrates. Gas hydrates are a frozen substance that forms under pressure when natural gas molecules, made up of mostly methane, are trapped in an envelope of water molecules.

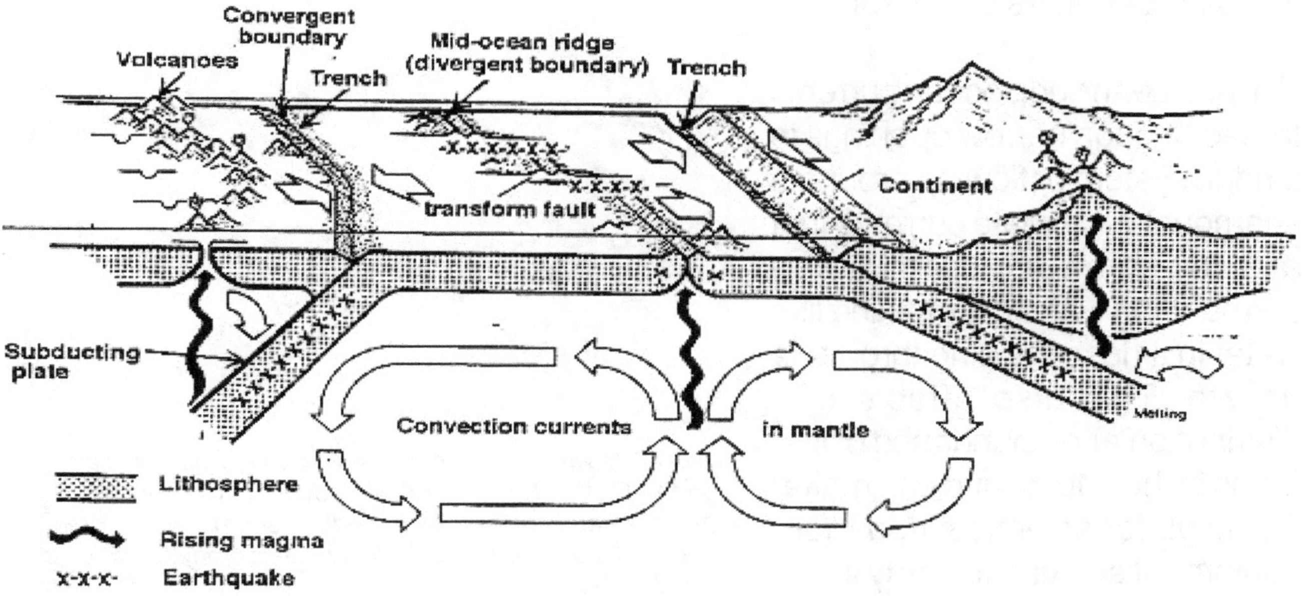

WHAT MAKES THE OCEAN WATER MOVE?

The water in the Oceans move, something like rivers, in Ocean currents. These currents are caused by the wind, density differences in water masses caused by temperature and salinity variations, gravity, and events such as earthquakes.

Surface currents are caused, almost entirely, by wind. The wave patterns on the surface of the water are determined by wind direction.

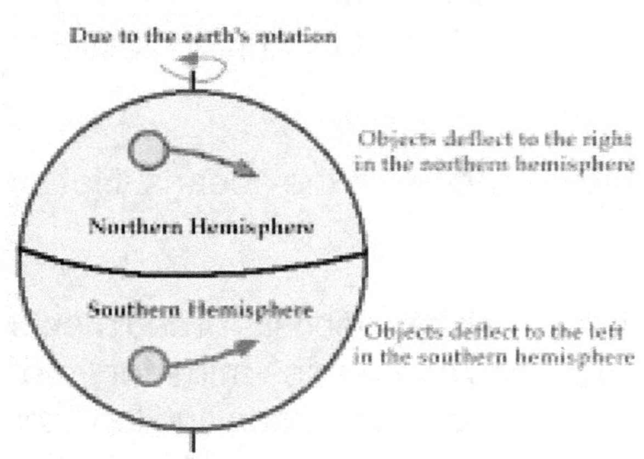

However, *Coriolis forces* (that is a term for you to look up) that result from the Earth's rotation, and the position of continents and other land masses interact with the currents blocking and redirecting them. Surface wind-driven currents in conjunction with landforms, and convection currents create deepwater currents like the famous Gulf Stream.

Bottom currents wipe and sort sediments which run off from land masses into the oceans and seas. This affects the type of plain that develops at the bottom of the water nearby the shore. It can be hard or soft, fine grained or coarse. Bottom material, called "substrate" then determines what types of habitat forms in that area for sea life.

When a current that is moving over a very large area is forced into a limited space, it usually becomes very strong.

On the ocean floor, ocean currents forced through narrow openings in a ridge system or flowing around a seamount can create currents that are far stronger than in the surrounding water (Something like water in a hose passing through a nozzle. This also affects the distribution and abundance of life forms in the habitat and can make it difficult for scientists and their equipment seeking to study it.

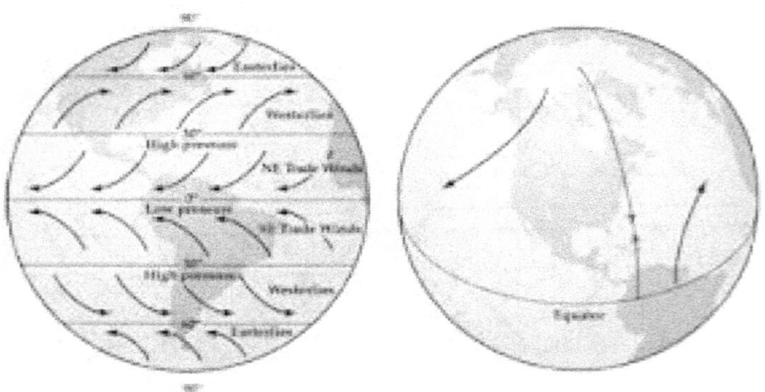

Prevailing winds change depending upon where you are on the Earth. The illustration above shows those winds as you change latitude from north to south. We learned about latitude and longitude in the Geography Continents workboook.

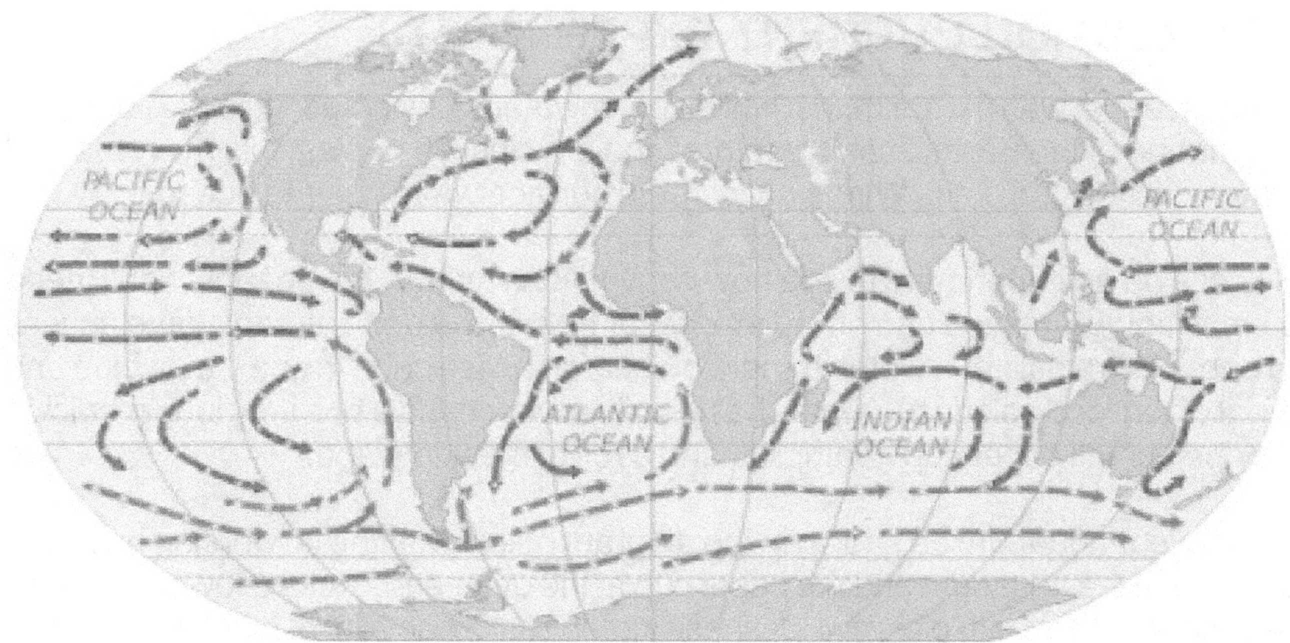

MAIN GLOBAL OCEAN CURRENT MAP

As I said, Ocean Currents happen because of density changes in the water.

The density of Water is affected by both temperature and salinity differences (the amount of chemical salts dissolved in the water).

These currents drive water masses through the deep Oceans and Seas and carry nutrients, oxygen, and heat along with them.

We learned about Convection Currents in the Earth's Mantle in the *Geography Continents* Workbook. These currents are responsible for the movement of the continental land masses on the Tetonic Plates holding the Continents and cause them to move very slowly over the planet.

But, convection currents do not just occur in liquid rock. All liquids and gasses can have currents because of differential heating. This includes water in the oceans.

Temperature also has an effect on water circulation. Less dense (lighter), warm liquid or gas rises while more dense (heavier) cool material sinks.

It is this movement that contributes greatly to circulation patterns of the Currents in the air or atmosphere and in water as well as in the Earth's Mantle.

CONVECTION CURRENT EXPERIMENT

In the oceans, warm water rises, while cooler water sinks creating flow. Along with the turning of the Earth, salinity factors, and physical obstacles, this movement of water creates currents. Winds only create surface waves on the ocean.

So, let's do an experiment to see how convection works in the oceans. You'll need a small aquarium (you can often get one for free, if you don't already have access to one, on Craigslist), a water immersion heater, an ice cube tray, a vial of blue and a vial of red food coloring, a turkey baster with rubber handle or a very long medicine dropper, small paper cup, toothpick, and a roll of masking tape.

Set up your aquarium as shown in the diagram below with the immersion heater at one end of the aquarium and the paper cup at the other end. Poke a few holes in the paper cup with a tooth pick, awl, or shesh kabob stick. Add a lot of blue food coloring to water in the ice tray. Make sure the water is a very dark blue. Then freeze the ice in the tray.

About an hour before you remove the ice cubes from the freezer, turn on the immersion heater in the aquarium. Obviously, you will have already filled the aquarium with water about three-quarters full. Be sure the heating element of the heater is under water and that the top of the paper cup is also slightly above the water level.

When the ice cubes are completely hardened, put them in the paper cup that you taped to the side of the aquarium. Then squirt out a few drops of red colored water at the bottom of the aquarium near the immersion heater.

Watch what happens through the glass side of the aquarium. Which icolor is denser and flows to the bottom of the tank and which color is lighter floating towards the surface?

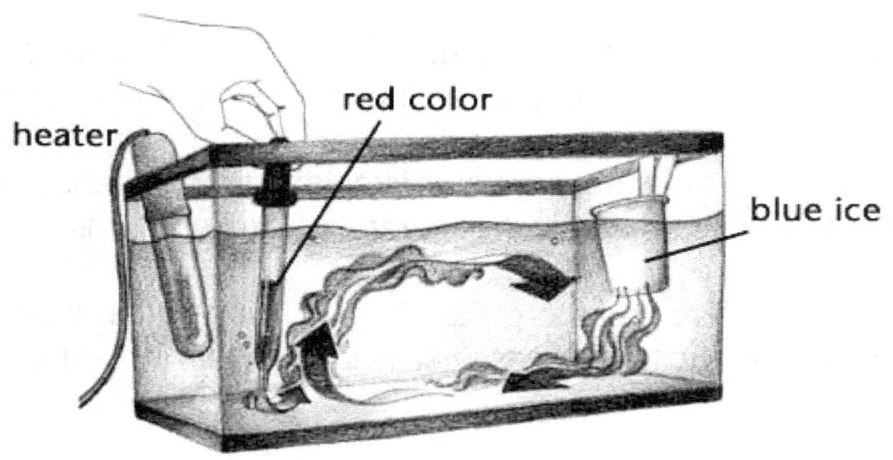

WHAT CAUSES THE TIDES?

Tides are rises and falls of the Oceans and Seas that happen every day.

Tides are caused mostly because of the gravity between the Earth and the Moon. The gravity around the Moon causes the water in the Oceans to extend towards the position of the Moon as it orbits around the Earth.

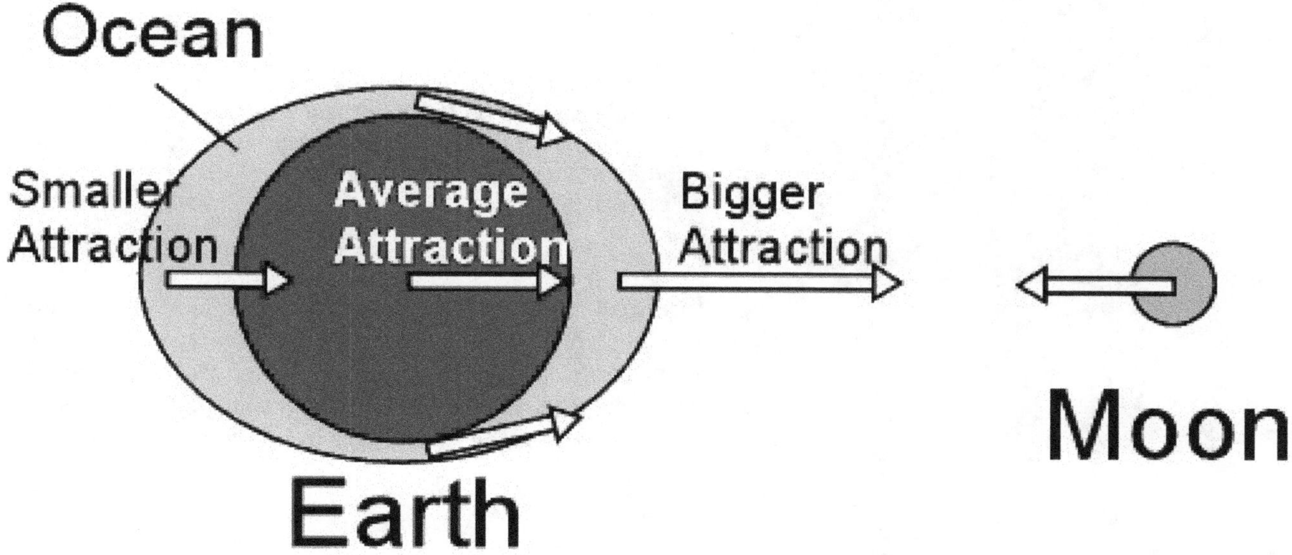

As the Earth rotates, the continental land masses of the Earth pass through both of these bulges each day because the Earth spins on its axis at a different rate than the Moon orbits around it.

When you're in one of the bulges of water, you experience a high tide. When you're not in one of the bulges, you go though a low tide. This cycle of two high tides and two low tides occurs days on most of the coastlines of the world. Sometimes greater in some places than others.

The Sun also causes tides just like the moon does, although the impact is not as great. This is because the Sun, although much larger than the Moon, is much farther away from the Earth.

Because the orbit of the Sun and Moon can be predicted, we can tell in advance when high and low tides will occur. As a result, sailors, fishermen, oceanographers, and other mariners use Tide Charts when they have to know when during the day these events will happen. Can you find Tide Charts for your area online or download a Tide Chart app for your cell phone or tablet?

Gravitational forces from both the sun and the moon continuously pull on the Earth. Although the moon is much smaller than the sun, the moon's gravity is the dominant force behind Earth's tides.

High Tide and Low Tide How high tides get and how often they occur depend on the position of the moon as it revolves around the Earth. The moon's pull is strongest on the part of the Earth directly facing the moon. When that part happens to be a part of the ocean, the water there bulges toward the moon.

When the Earth, Moon, and Sun all line up (this happens during the Full Moon and New Moon) the gravity of the Sun abd Moon adds to each other, so the tides (called Spring Tides) are higher than regular tides.

There is a new moon or a full moon every fourteen (14) days or so. Thus, that's how often we see the higher Spring Tides.

When gravity of the Sun and Moon acts against each other, the tides are usually lower than normal. These are called "Neap Tides."

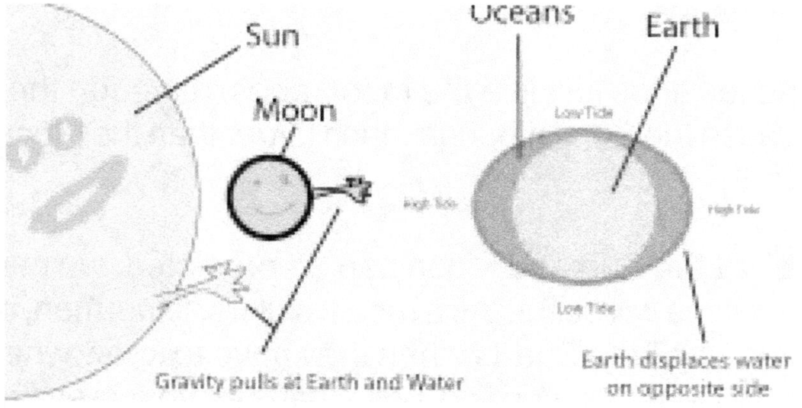

COLOR THE LIGHTHOUSE

COLOR THE SEASHORE

WHAT CAUSES WAVES?

Waves are moving peaks or "Crest" and valleys or "Troughs" between them.

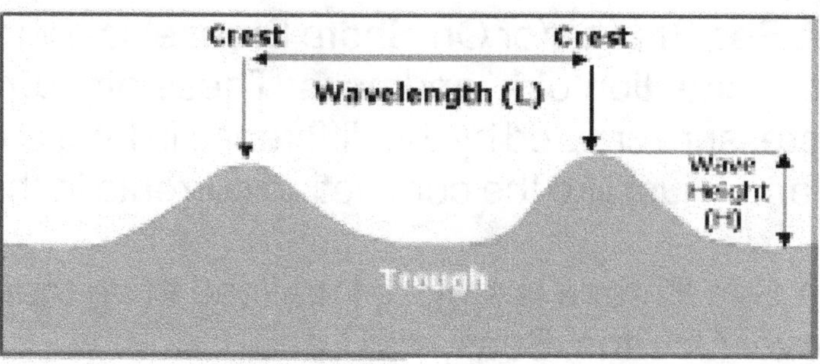

A Crest is the highest point the water reaches and the Trough is the lowest point the water reaches on the surface of the Ocean or Sea.

Waves are usually caused by wind transferring its energy to the Ocean's surface. These waves or "Swells" can travel over very long distances.

A wave's size depends on the speed of the wind, the duration that the wind blows, and the amount of area over which the wind is blowing.

Underwater earthquakes or landslides can cause huge Tsunamis or Tidal Waves. These can move water a great distance inland when they reach shallow areas and coastlines because waves get magnified in height as the sea bottom gets closer to the water's surface. Tidal waves are often very distructive.

Breaking Waves

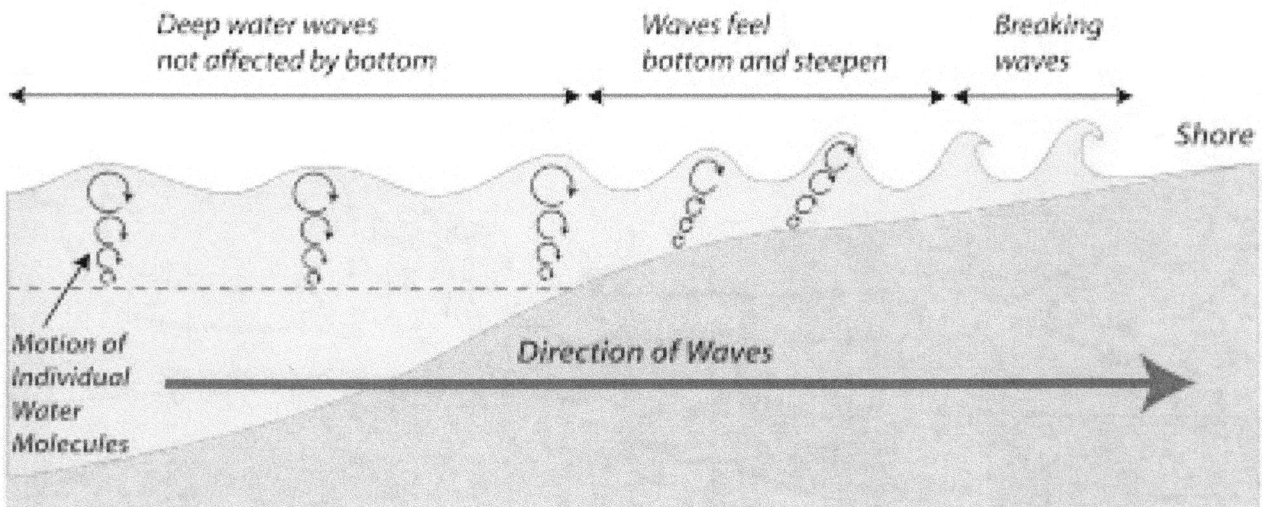

WHY IS IT OFTEN WINDY AT THE BEACH?

A Sea Breeze (or On-Shore Breeze) is a wind that blows from the Ocean or Sea in the direction of a landmass. These air currents develop due to differences in air pressure created by the difference in heat contained in the water and that on the dry land -- just like the convection currents in the water itself.

A Sea Breeze is a more localised thing than Prevailing Wind that otherwise flows over Oceans, Seas, and Land.

SInce the Land absorbs radiation from the Sun a lot more quickly than water will, a Sea Breeze is common along coastal areas after sunrise.

Dry Land cools more quickly than water does. So, after dark, a Land Breeze (or Offshore Breeze) has the reverse effect.

Thus, a Sea Breeze tends to dissipate after sunset and the wind will turn around and Blow from the land towards the Ocean or Sea.

COLOR THE CASTAWAY

COLOR THE CORAL REEF

MAKE A SEA SHELL MOBILE

Seashells are a hard, outer cover created by an animal that lives in the sea that protects the animal's soft insides.

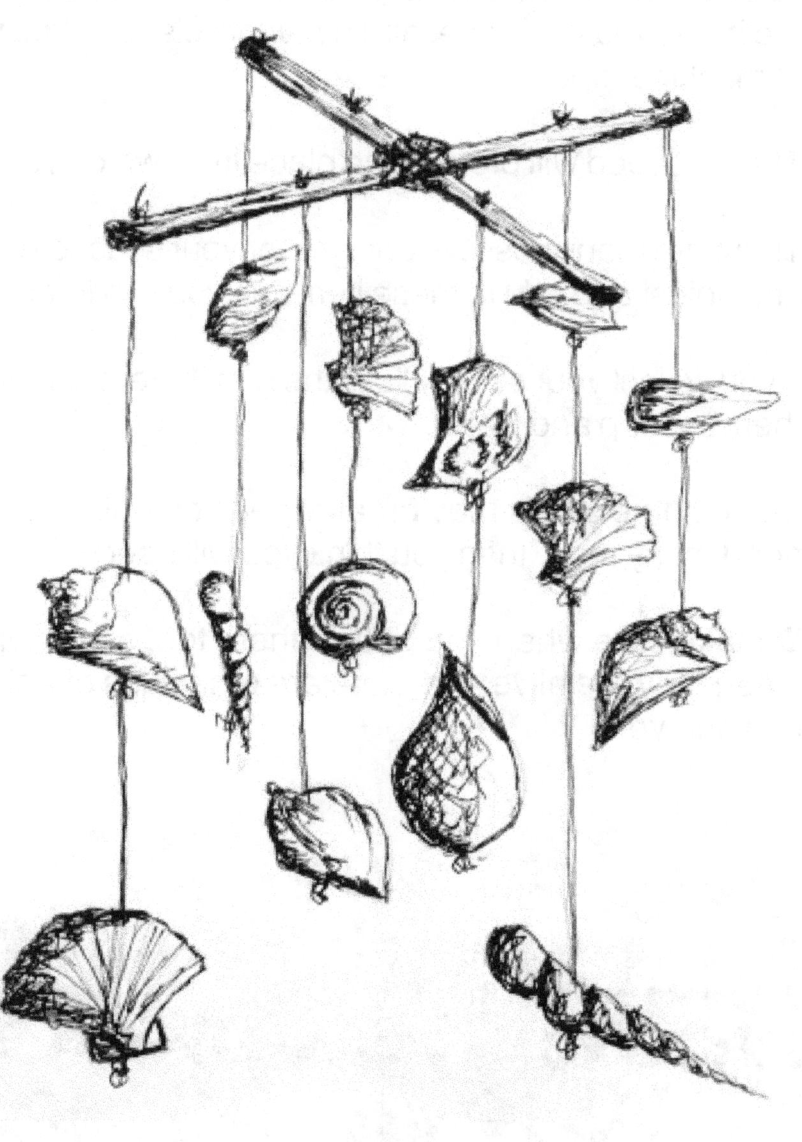

When the animal dies and the soft parts have been eaten by another animal or have rotted away, the empty seashell often washes up on the shoreline where it can be found and collected by beachcombers.

Seashells are composed of a chemical called calcium carbonate which is secreted by the mollusk from which the seashell comes. When empty, these shells can make a beautiful display.

A wind chime made out of seashells is a simple and inexpensive project to remember a beach vacation or to simply pass the time while learning about different sea creatures.

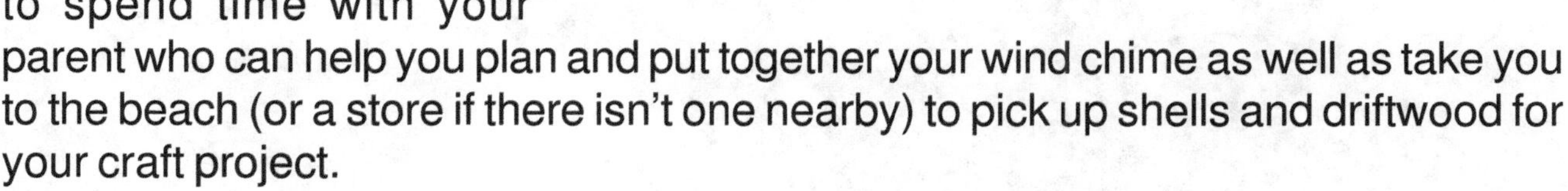

This project is also a fun way to spend time with your parent who can help you plan and put together your wind chime as well as take you to the beach (or a store if there isn't one nearby) to pick up shells and driftwood for your craft project.

This activity requires a few tools and materials that you may need your parent to help you with or supervise you as you use them. But, even if you need some help, you will have a lot of leeway in crafting your own uniquue design decisions to create a seashell wind chime that makes a fine addition to your room decor.

First, you are going to need to collect all your materials.

You'll need at least 24 nice large shells, a piece or two of driftwood, some hemp string (you can also use strong fishing line), a drill or Dremel Tool with a small size ceramic drill bit and a small wood bit large enough to allow thye string to pass through the holes you will make, and a pair of scissors. You will also need a pencil and a roll of masking tape.

The driftwood will provide the place from which you will hang your shell chimes.

There are many possible designs for your seashell wind chime. Use your imagination and adjust and add to these items as you find interesting things as you beachcomb.

If you collect your seashells at the beach, remember to clean them well before using them in soap and water.

Since some shells may break when you drill them, it's a good idea to gather up a good many more than you think you will need.

Do take care when you gather them too, some types of shell fish are poisonous when they are alive and there are other kids of animals on or near the beach than can hurt you.

The driftwoof will be the piece from which you will hang your seashells. So, when you get back home, the next thing you need to do is to prepare your driftwood to hold the strings on which your shell selections will hang.

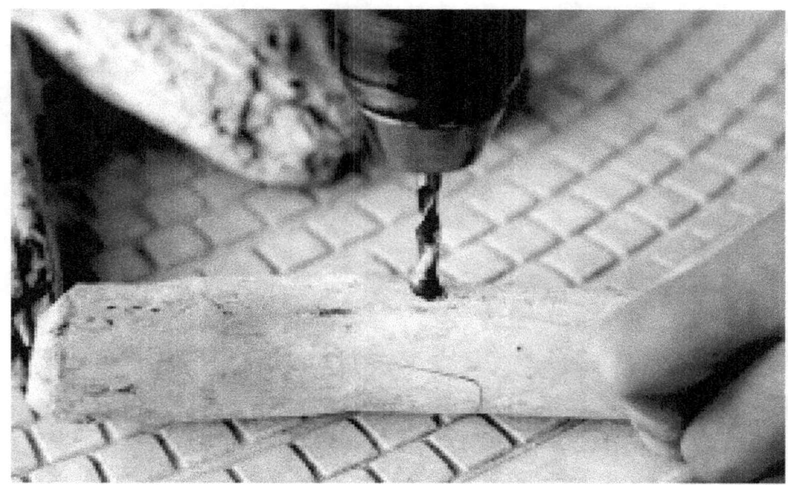

Begin by drilling holes into the driftwood so that you can pass the string through and tie it off at the top.

Place the driftwood on a flat surface and use a pencil to mark out evenly spaced points along its length to hold the strings about 2 to 3 inches apart. Be sure that your marks are consistantly spaced and along the topmost edge so that when you drill through the driftwood the holes are parallel to each other.

Attach the wood drill bit to your drill and make holes along its length. The holes must be large enough to pass your string or fishing line through them.

If you are using more than one piece of driftwood for your wind chime, connect the additional pieces of driftwood together to complete your mounting frame.

Then prepare the seashells that you are going to hang from the string. The shells should be string between 1 and 2 inches apart.

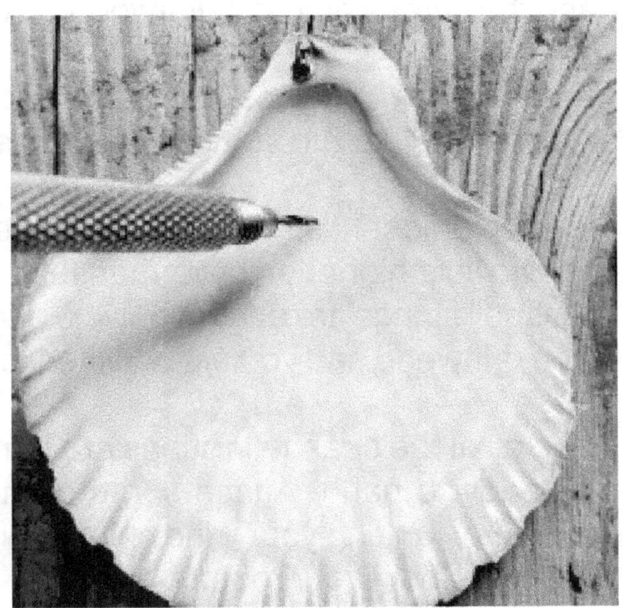

Using the ceramic drill bit, drill a hole through each seashell at the top of the shell or some convenient place that will make it eash to string the shell.

To help prevent the shell from breaking, put a piece of masking tape over the hole's location before drilling.

Once the hole is drilled, remove the tape carefully.

The next step is to cut your string into the number of pieces that you require for your wind chime design. The pieces need to be at least 30 inches long. Tie each string through the holes you drilled in each seashell and make a large knot to keep the shell from shifting along the string. Leave at least 6 inches of string at the top of each strand.

Tie as many shells as you can on each string placing them 1 or 2 inches apart. Then trim off any excess string so that the last shell in the line has the last knot at the bottom of each string.

Once all of your shells have been attached to the pieces of string, you are ready to hang the strings onto the driftwood pieces.

Then hang the strings containing the seashells from the driftwood and knot the string at the top so that the strings are secure.

Tie each adjacent string of shells to the driftwood, positioning the strand so that it hangs a little higher or lower than the one next to it and repeat this pricess until all your shell strings are attached to the driftwood frame. Once all of the strings are tied to the driftwood and you are satisfied, cut off the excess string using your scissors.

Once all of the seashells stings are hanging from the driftwood, your wind chimes are ready to hang. Attach some of the string you have left to the driftwood as necessary to hang your wind chime from a hook in the ceiling or eave area outside your home or in your room.

OCEANS CROSSWORD PUZZLE

Down:
1. A jagged rock or coral just above or below the surface of a body of water
2. A building that contains a beacon of light to warn ships of dangerous waters
3. A salt water cove separated from the sea by a low sandbank or coral reef
7. A vast body of salt water
8. A flow of water moving in a specific direction
9. A large area of salt water located where land and ocean meet
10. The place where land meets a body of water
12. A body of water forming an inlet in the shoreline that is larger than a cove but smaller than a gulf

Across:
4. the area of water where the salt water tide of the sea meets the fresh water of the river
5. A deep area of the salt water almost surrounded by land with a narrow mouth
6. A narrow passage of water between sections of land leading to a bay or lagoon
11. A deposit of sand that forms a shallow area in body of water
13. A long ripple on the surface of water that curls into an arch
14. A sheltered body of water smaller than a Bay
15. A fixed float to mark a reef or other hazard or for mooring a boat
16. The rising and falling of a sea or ocean caused by the attraction of the moon and

CROSSWORD PUZZLE ANSWERS

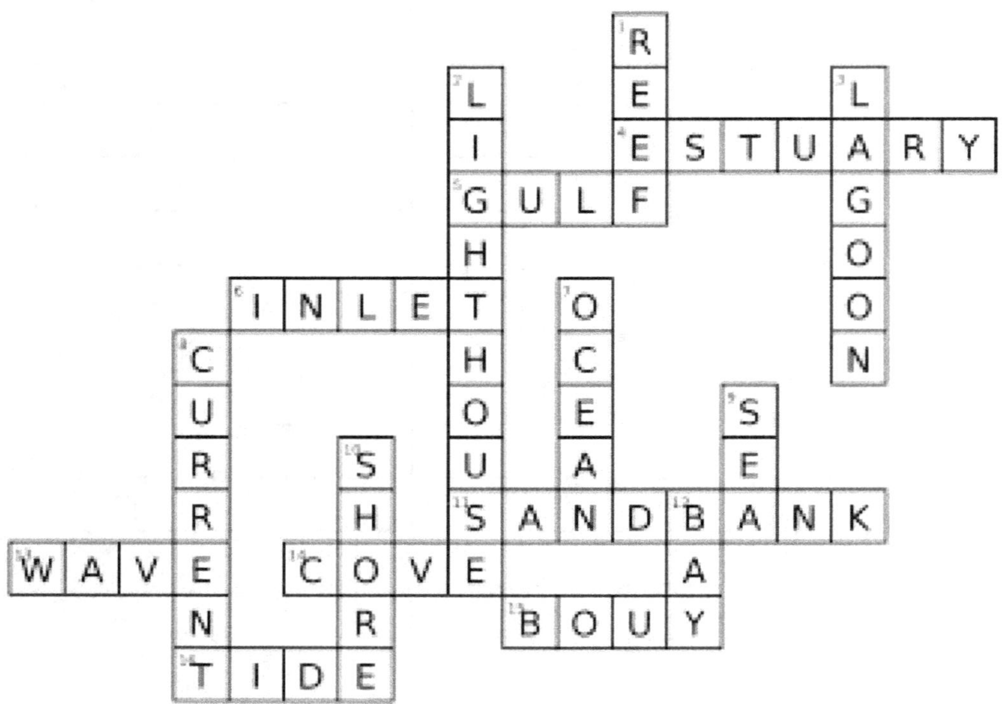

Down:

1. A jagged rock or coral just above or below the surface of a body of water
2. A building that contains a beacon of light to warn ships of dangerous waters
3. A salt water cove separated from the sea by a low sandbank or coral reef
7. A vast body of salt water
8. A flow of water moving in a specific direction
9. A large area of salt water located where land and ocean meet
10. The place where land meets a body of water
12. A body of water forming an inlet in the shoreline that is larger than a cove but smaller than a gulf

Across:

4. the area of water where the salt water tide of the sea meets the fresh water of the river
5. A deep area of the salt water almost surrounded by land with a narrow mouth
6. A narrow passage of water between sections of land leading to a bay or lagoon
11. A deposit of sand that forms a shallow area in body of water
13. A long ripple on the surface of water that curls into an arch
14. A sheltered body of water smaller than a Bay
15. A fixed float to mark a reef or other hazard or for mooring a boat
16. The rising and falling of a sea or ocean caused by the attraction of the moon and

COLOR THE PORPOISES

LIFE IN THE OCEANS AND SEAS

Billions of plants and animals make their homes in the Oceans and Seas.

Most live only near surface where sunlight can reach them. Some life forms are so small you need a microscope to see them. Others grow as very large. The giant blue whale is the largest animal on Earth today. Oceanographers organize, or "classify" marine life into the same two primary groups we know on land: plants and animals.

Ocean Plants

Plankton grows mostly near the surface of the Ocean or Sea and is affected by how much sunlight it receives. It also needs nutrients which dissolve in the water and is carried up from the bottom of the Ocean or Sea by Currents.

As you can see, not all Ocean or Sea dwelling plants have roots like those found on the land. Some, like Plankton, simply drift around in the water while other rooted plants can only be found in shallow water. This is because there there would not be enough sunlight to sustain them in deep water where the sunlight can't reach them.

Sunlight can't reach depths greater than a few hundred feet below the Ocean or Sea. Therefore, the vast majority of the Oceans are not able to support plants that have roots -- like kelp (a kind of seaweed). But, you will find non-rooted plants all over the Ocean's surface water.

Ocean Animals

Although adapted to life in the Ocean, many of the same types of animals live in the Oceans and Seas as live on land. These include air breathing mammals and reptiles

like turtles. In addition, Oceans and Seas are home to all sorts of fish, crustacians (crabs, lobsters, shrimp for example), Cephalopods (such as octopus, squid, and cuttlefish) and many other creatures that evolved in water.

Some birds, although usually air dwelling, live near the Oceans and Seas because they feed on animals that live in or near salt water.

In fact, scientists believe that all life on Earth had its beginnings in the Oceans.

The Ocean Food Chain

All living organisms can only survive if they eat some king of food. The Food Chain is a series of steps by which the energy of the sun and inorganic chemicals is transferred from one organism to another.

Through the process of photosynthesis, plants manufacture organic food from water, carbon dioxide, and other chemical nutrients using sunlight as their source of energy to convert those elements into simple carbohydrates that comprise their food.

Animals have to obtain food from other living organisms.

So, the bottom of the "Food Chain" in the Oceans is a plant known as "Plankton." Like all plants, Plankton requires sunlight to live. They are very simple, single-cell algae, a kind of plankton, that some smaller animals consume as food. As you already know, animals that eat plants are Herbivores. Not all Herbivores that live in the Oceans or Seas are small. Some of the biggest animals in the Oceans are Herbivores.

Carnivores are preditors that hunt for and consume other animals rather than make food for themselves. Fish that eat other animals -- like sharks and other preditory fish are Carnivores. So are octopus, squid, and many other sea creatures. Omnivores are creatures that eat both plants or other animals.

Some ocean animals are scavengers that will eat any of the leftovers that Carnivores and Omnivores don't finish and organisms that die naturally.

In the end, you can trace what each animal eats back to the plants that produce organic materials from the sun and inorganic chemicals they ingest.

THE OCEAN FOOD CHAIN

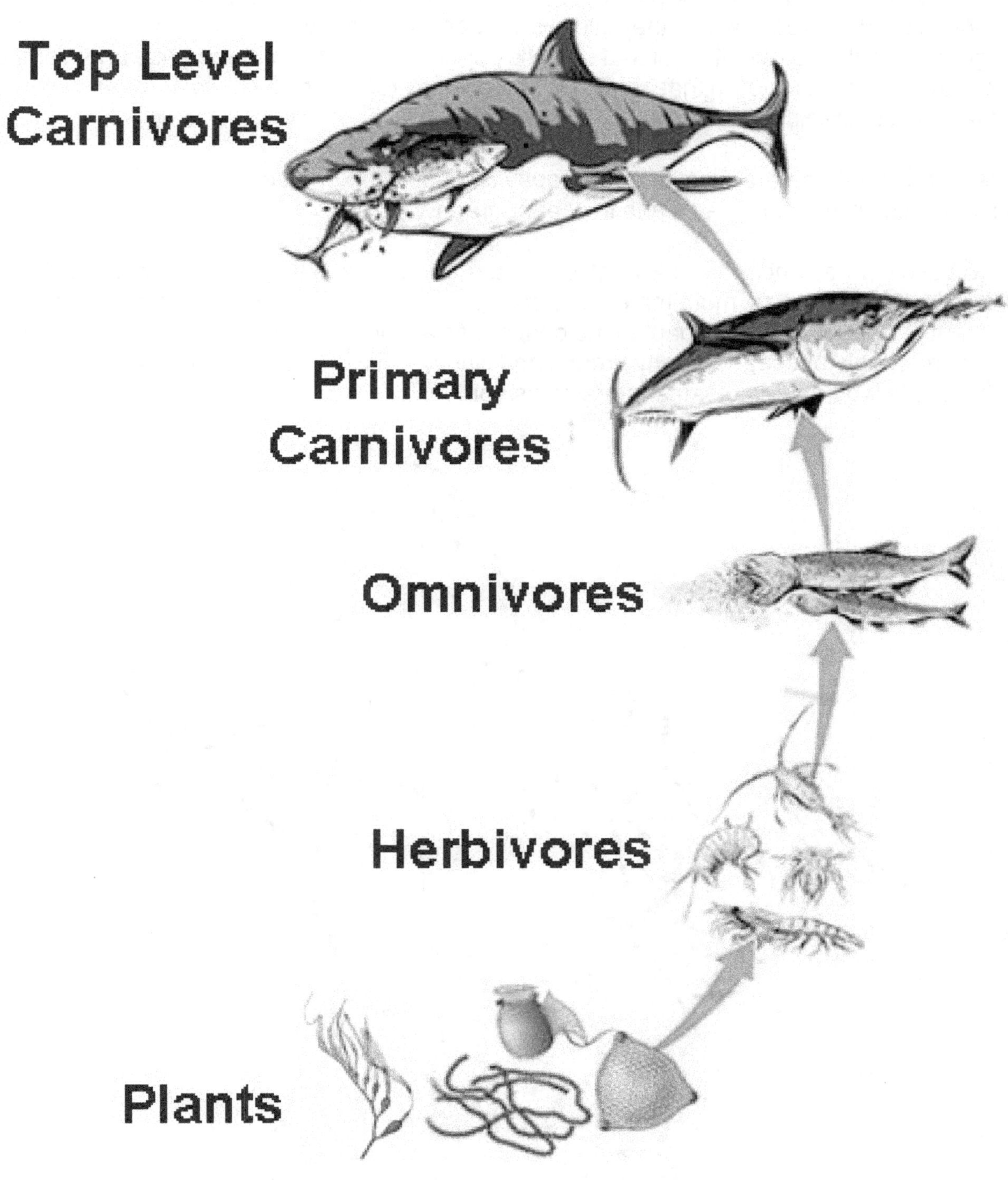

A FINAL THOUGHT

How does living near the Ocean or Sea impact people who reside there? Does it have an effect on how they behave. What they eat? How they socialize? What kinds of animals and plants live near the sea or in it? What is the weather like near the ocean or sea?

The oceans and seas and how people relate to them are reflected in the cultures of the inhabitants of the area in which they live. How does their history, local culture, socio-economy, language and the composition of that specific population. Impact, characterize and identify an average person who lives in that area? Do you see any relationship between these factors that make local cultures unique?

Questions like these are what oceanography is all about! You see, there is a wide variety of scientific disciplines that play a role in oceanography.

If you have learned enough in this booklet to interest you in studying oceanography further, you should look for, and read, more material that will provide you with insights as to how people from different regions in of world adapt to the challenges associated with living where they do. You should also look for oceanography groups and clubs, and travel to meet others and learn more from people who have the same interests as you.

ABOUT THE AUTHOR

Scott Marlowe studied education at Polk Community College, anthropology at the Florida Keys Community College and majored in the social sciences at Rollins College.

Between educational endeavors, Scott traveled the world extensively pursuing paleontology, archeology,and anthropologhy disciplines. His extensive field work experience gives his academic understanding considerable depth and a strong appreciation of a practical, hands-on approach to instruction in combination with conventional classroom learning.

Scott began teaching in 1978. His first teaching position was instructing art and design in the adult education program for Fairfax County, Virginia at Thomas Edison High School. By 1980 Scott was teaching design at the Northern Virginia Community College, Louden County, Virginia Campus.In 1981.

After moving back to Central Florida in 1995, Scott established, and began teaching, a successful high school level, school-to-work program for the Lake Alfred Career Development Center.

Scott retired in 2001 due to a physical disability. However, he accepted a position teaching high school students at the Polk Youth Development Center where he again demonstrated the value of computer technology in education. Scott remained at PYDC until 2003 when the facility changed management.

Scott became involved in Florida Paleontology as a volunteer and field guide for the Graves Museum where he performed fossil restoration in the paleo-lab and conducted expeditions to the top fossil hunting locations in the state.

Leading organizations around the world now recognize Scott's expertise in fossil sites

located in the State of Florida. Scott was selected by the French National Museum of Natural History to conduct a group of their researchers around the Florida Peninsula to collect specimens for the museum's collections and research center. This group discovered a new species of cancellaria while on expedition with Scott a few years ago and the museum group is sending representatives to again tour Florida fossil beds with Scott in 2009.

Edward Petuch, the popular marine paleontogist responsible to many scholarly works on Florida's fossil molluska named a new species he discovered in Marlowe's honor.

Scott continues advancing educational programs and objectives at Pangea Institute and is the author of the highly popular fossil field guides "Florida Fossils."